WET

WICK POETRY FIRST BOOK SERIES
David Hassler, Editor

Wet

Poems by

Carolyn Creedon

The Kent State University Press

Kent, Ohio

© 2012 by Carolyn Creedon
All rights reserved
Library of Congress Catalog Card Number 2012013503
ISBN 978-1-60635-150-5
Manufactured in the United States of America

The Wick Poetry Series is sponsored by the Stan and Tom Wick Poetry Center and the Department of English at Kent State University.

LIBRARY OF CONGRESS CATALOGING-IN-PUBLICATION DATA
Creedon, Carolyn.
Wet : poems / by Carolyn Creedon.
    p.   cm.
"The Wick Poetry First Book Series."
ISBN 978-1-60635-150-5 (pbk. : alk. paper) ∞
I. Title.
PS3603.R446W48 2012
811'.6—dc22   2012013503

16 15 14 13 12   5 4 3 2 1

"I feel like a wet seed wild in the hot blind earth."

—*William Faulkner*

CONTENTS

III.

"I want to leak all over the world, / the wet and tilted wheel," Carolyn Creedon declares in the title poem of her fierce and unflinching first book, *Wet*. "I want you to see that I am who / I say I am," she says, "an unsavory woman with her seasons undone."

I was immediately arrested by the seasoned voice in *Wet*, the Plathean directness of the speaker, a woman who writes out of the body, out of lived experience, no holds barred, and refuses to prettify things, as in the splendid one-sentence poem, "Woman, Mined," that cleverly begins the book:

> In the cosmetics department of Lord & Taylor
> they'll take you right there, right out in the open,
> plain as day, and snap you with an ultraviolet camera,
> show what you've done to your skin just
> by living, your face exposed suddenly like what's
> really going on under a lifted-up log, the real you
> you are, caught and pinned like a moth,
> like a shoplifter, like a woman on a table . . .

The cosmetics department of a department store suddenly seems like an illicit place because of what it exposes, how a woman has aged, what she has done to herself over the years simply by living. Creedon likes to build a strong rhythm in a poem, to sweep us along on the music of her associations, letting a literal situation yield up its metaphorical power, and this lyric, which reminds me of Randall Jarrell's poem "The Face," crescendos *end ?* with the lines "and you'll wear your face / with its amber earned, its amethyst, its intaglio tear- / etched diamond, and say, *I am cut that way*."

Creedon writes litanies and traditional forms, such as the sonnet ("The Shift," "A Water Sonnet," "Holding") and the sestina ("Just a Sestina to you, Honey . . ."), which she invests with vernacular energy. She updates nursery rhymes ("Shoe, Worn") and mythological stories ("Medusa's Sisters," "Medusa's Love Song," "Doris"), and talks back to traditional poems, such as Hopkins' "Pied Beauty." She speaks bluntly, when necessary ("For Jill, Who's Blue on Account of She Just Broke Up With Her Lover, an Asshole Doctor from Across the Water") and creates her own mock instruction manuals ("How to Be a Cowgirl in a Studio Apartment"), one of which, "Wet 2.0," ends with a jaunty credo:

> And now you (because what in this good and green earth
> have I to protect you from) want to know why I'm made of wet?
> I'm made of mother, baby. Come on,
>   let me show you
>   my beautiful filth.

One of the greatest strengths of this radically engendered book is its portraits of women, ordinary working women, who turn out to be extraordinary. There is "Michelle" and "ganges Ophelia," the working women in "Whore" and the girl in "Fireflies" ("She is lit up inside just like the fireflies, just like a spangly harem / dancer or a string of Christmas lights"). Creedon has clearly spent a lot of time working in restaurants and bars, and she makes the most of it here. One thinks, amongst others, of the waitress in "Fillmore and Geary," the bartender in "The Rusty Nail" ("her face / laced with those lines the finger strokes of work, / of winey evenings, of half—bad luck, of the cool hustle of loving / too much and not getting that back exactly the way she served it / up"), and the exhausted veteran in "Permanent" ("It's cold enough outside that she wants to put her face / inside a waffle iron and plug it in. All she wants to do / is get home. She's thirty-six. She's a thousand years old").

I'm moved by the way that Carolyn Creedon's work treats experience as sacred. She won't look away from difficult truths. She writes frankly about her own frustrations, longings, and heartbreaks, but she also recognizes the suffering of others—their secret grievances and griefs. The daily working world is here in full measure. And yet there's an oddly religious feeling that keeps breaking through this volume, which cherishes the small things, the lesser divinities, and ends with a prayer. It heartens me to welcome this fiery and fervent book, this wet collection, into the world.

I.

WOMAN, MINED

In the cosmetics department of Lord & Taylor
they'll take you right there, right out in the open,
plain as day, and snap you with an ultraviolet camera,
show you what you've done to your skin just
by living, your face exposed suddenly like what's
really going on under a lifted-up log, the real you
you are, caught and pinned like a moth,
like a shoplifter, like a woman on a table

and the lady in the crisp white smock will expertly
flick the snapshot in front of you, laid out
like a color-coded map of conquered countries,
the purples and browns places you gave up
without a care in your twenties, to late nights
and poolside deck chairs and men, all the men
you touched, the ones who marked you, whose traces
you bear, and now you can see the archaeology
of tears, their white-acid trails, and the lady
will say, sternly, *Look what you did*
      ← — Future ! cool !

and you will see the mess of it you made, and you
will see the times when you carelessly went to bed
with someone without the proper moisturizer, when you
suckled that man like a baby, and when you moved
with another like a girl on a rocker until you fell off
and lost him, and finally picked another, like the best-of-all
flower, and kept him, cried on him, made him sandwiches,
made him a baby, and you'll wear your face   / Q
with its amber earned, its amethyst, its intaglio tear-
etched diamond, and say, *I am cut that way.*

MEDUSA'S SISTERS

Two sisters drank all day in a cave and shared one eye, cackling
and passing it around like a joint at a party. At night, they made dolls
from piles of stolen socks. Come one hot night, a beautiful furry man
flew in like an angora bat. He promised them a feather from each foot
if he could just see the slimy eye. He was charming. They were lonely.
They all drank a little too much Baileys. They let him see.
There was the sound of beating feet against the mouth of the cave.
He was gone. They were forgotten. They couldn't see.
They held each other's faces and tried to weep. — *No eyes*

HOW TO BE A COWGIRL IN A STUDIO APARTMENT

Paint the ceiling blue and let it dry. See pamphlet "How to Paint a Ceiling."
Chalk a large circle to represent the sun. A light bulb will do as well.
Start close to the sun and trace Mercury. Trace each planet. Finish with Pluto.
Pour each color into a plastic container. Paint each planet and the sun.

—from anonymous pamphlet, "How to Paint
the Solar System on Your Ceiling"

Don't let the people at Ace Hardware tell you you need a man.
Do pick one up anyway, if he looks red and ripe. A cowgirl needs
nourishment, and some nights, to lie on her back and let something
bloom above her, looming like the stars. A cowgirl's hardware
is indispensable—big-spurred boots, canteen, and a saddle to go—
useful, but always that soft underbelly she won't be revealing.
No need for the little black dress: a flannel shirt, jeans, a steaming
pan of wieners, and some bourbon. And him, over there. "Hey You!"
He'll come over. He'll have to. You're a renegade, a rough rider, a rogue
   feeling.
Paint the ceiling blue and let it dry. See pamphlet "How to Paint a Ceiling."

Get him there. Rein him in a little; don't let him roam too much.
You're well schooled in herding. Circle him, if you must, with a lasso,
then lead him—carry him, if you must, over one shoulder—over
his objections, over a bottle of wine, to the bed. Make him docile.
Hum like a whittled banjo. It helps if you know how to pet a wild
animal, or how to rub two sticks together with your hands, or shell
peanuts husk by husk—cowgirl skills that will come in handy when
rustling up blades of grass to whistle on, or handling unpredictable
forces that scare so easily. Undo his fly. Make him rise and swell.
Chalk a large circle to represent the sun. A light bulb will do as well.

Remember, he's borrowed, cowgirl; you don't buy things, the stars
you ride under slide over you like yellow peanuts, the big sky just
a rented ceiling, the big sun a borrowed bulb, a giant library card

from God. The planets unmoored are not your marbles, and the warm
man you rolled with, rode and sweated with, will go back to his natural
habitat, glistening wet. This is your rule: the cowgirl's status quo.
Bowls are only good for what they hold, branches for the scratch they
itch, stones for chalking circles of the light. Even your rope just
rings out the moon, your banjo mouth twangs out a temporary tempo.
Start close to the sun and trace Mercury. Trace each planet. Finish with
    Pluto.

Mark out the man. Trace him with your tongue like an outline of the
    moon
made of milk. You're a cowgirl. Circle him like you would a wild bull
in a cloud of red dust. Then let your wanting run, turn it over like a
    bucket
of color, let it spill into the other, and, panting, let it dry until it's done.
    Then
let him go. Untie the steed, neighing softly and nosing the shag-carpet
    tumbleweeds
beneath the semiglossed glow. Mosey into the kitchenette, holster your
    gun.
Ride the man gently back home, to whatever field or farm or store you
    stole
him from. Leave him there, with the other sticky objects: the marbles,
    the broken-
up pieces of stars, the rolling painted circles, fading into sky, one by one.
Pour each color into a plastic container. Paint each planet and the sun.

6

PAP

The whole thing was necessary. But for me,
up here on the third floor, each nerve
every day already humming down each synapse
give me valium like prisoners banging their trays,
a song on steel, it was hardly the thing.
But it was what to do, and needed, the goddamn
deck was falling to pieces, rotted from the inside
out so that each day I listen to the workers walk through
my living room, all whistles and Budweisers and dusty
boots, and hammers and miter saws that dive in
like bees, and it really was necessary, what shouldn't have
been there, what is rotting, or written on a womb like
a word, or a doctor's number a year ago on a card
I never called, whose name I don't remember
though he went right through me but didn't get it
all, sewed me crooked, washed me almost clean
like a dress with a wine stain, or a sweater in danger
from one loose thread. It really was necessary. I miss
that goddamn deck. I want to ask you if you miss it
out of me, if I am the same, if I am still necessary, if
I am still here. I sing something half-remembered to drown
the sounds of the men and the saws and all the things that are
almost all there. I sing to sink the wreck.

shift from description to metaphor

This one has the insecurity and dependency of traditional sex roles

LITANY

Tom, will you let me love you in your restaurant?
I will let you make me a sandwich of your invention and I will eat it
    and call
it a carolyn sandwich. Then you will kiss my lips and taste the mayon-
    naise and
that is how you shall love me in my restaurant

Tom, will you come to my empty beige apartment and help me set up
    my daybed?
Yes, and I will put the screws in loosely so that when we move on it, later,
it will rock like a cradle and then you will know you are my baby

Tom, I am sitting on my dirt bike on the deck. Will you come out from
    the kitchen
and watch the people with me?
Yes, and then we will race to your bedroom. I will win and we will
    tangle up
on your comforter while the sweat rains from our stomachs and fore-
    heads

Tom, the stars are sitting in tonight like gumball gems in a little girl's
jewelry box. Later can we walk to the duck pond?
Yes, and we can even go the long way past the jungle gym. I will push
    you on
the swing, but promise me you'll hold tight. If you fall I might disappear

Tom, can we make a baby together? I want to be a big pregnant woman
    with a
loved face and give you a squalling red daughter.
No, but I will come inside you and you will be my daughter

Tom, will you stay the night with me and sleep so close that we are one
    person?
No, but I will lie down on your sheets and taste you. There will be feathers
of you on my tongue and then I will never forget you

8

Tom, when we are in line at the convenience store can I put my hands in your
back pockets and my lips and nose in your baseball shirt and feel the crook
of your shoulder blade?
No, but later you can lie against me and almost touch me and when I go I will
leave my shirt for you to sleep in so that always at night you will be pressed
up against the thought of me

Tom, if I weep and want to wait until you need me will you promise that someday
you will need me?
No, but I will sit in silence while you rage, you can knock the chairs down
any mountain. I will always be the same and you will always wait

Tom, will you climb on top of the dumpster and steal the sun for me? It's just
hanging there and I want it.
No, it will burn my fingers. No one can have the sun: it's on loan from God.
But I will draw a picture of it and send it to you from Richmond and then you
can smooth out the paper and you will have a piece of me as well as the sun

Tom, it's so hot here, and I think I'm being born. Will you come back from
Richmond and baptise me with sex and cool water?
I will come back from Richmond. I will smooth the damp spiky hairs from the
back of your neck and then I will lick the salt off it. Then I will leave

Tom, Richmond is so far away. How will I know how you love me?
I have left you. That is how you will know

RADISH

Everywhere you look there are children, unkempt, top-heavy,
wild-fronded radishes in a garden that only grows radishes;
there they are, in line, at the store, on the street,
whinging out a sticky song of want, thumbs red, enlarged
and teethed, moist bottoms mired flat to where other people
eat, a steady stream, a boiling out, of snot and piss and
greed. Everywhere you go

people love children, I suppose because everyone knows,
or was, or has one these days, everyone eager to hear
the clever things they say, eager to see some stranger's
photos of their seed launched, ejaculated from a loaded
wallet, spilling out for all the world to see, these midgets,
these laminated soldiers, marching perforated, jackbooted,
mary-janed, a staccato gunshot stream. I like children (I like to say)

slow roasted, on a spit. The marrow is the best
that way (I'll mention), just to shock, just for spite,
just to stick it to the ones who think they have the right to ask.
Lately, everywhere I'm at, people look askance; I'm hoping
one day to be that old lady in the A-frame just out of town
whose legend grows with each legion of children who whisper,
ring her doorbell, run away. The fact is children frighten me,
what they are asking of me, at once smooth-faced, guileless,
wobbly as eggs; at once a parade of necessities, of bathroom
breaks, of sunburn block, of brought-up memories, of need.

The A-frame was an easy walk over the Narragansett rocks
from our rental house, nobody wanted it because nobody
ever lived there, but I wanted never to leave, with its one eye
boarded up with a wink, its frame named A for how its head poked
into the sun, I wanted to be in there forever (years later, pregnant
by a man who couldn't look at me, I thought of it still
there, not mine, but no one else's either) even knowing I had to go home
—there was a girl named Radish, my mother whispers over and over,

with red hair like yours, she had many adventures—I think that I will never
live there, my mother has put a puppy in the oven to warm, it came out
of its mother cold and still, comes out of the oven gasping for air. Its mother
licks it clean and whole. I find my mother's cardigan draped like an empty skin
over her purse. I press it over my mouth and nose. Breathe in
camphor, Desitin, cigarettes, the ocean, me.

THE SHIFT

Back when I began to need desperately to see
how you saw me (a year ago? last week?), after the rift,
after the time of lazy flannel shirts I'd wear that you'd lift
up and burrow in like you were climbing inside me,
you gave me an antique nightie (a prize, a parting gift?),
someone else's lingerie, and though she was very probably
dead, still, she was obviously thinner, and attractively dainty
(and oh yeah, not me), so I tried to try on this shift.
But the bodice ripped open with jagged alacrity;
out sprang a breast like a starfish all on its own
with startled, blinking, just-awake opacity,
onto my shore as if unstuck from a stone,
awkward, surprised at its own hot-pink audacity,
fanned out helplessly, dumbly searching, suddenly alone.

PERMANENT

It's cold enough outside that she wants to put her face
inside a waffle iron and plug it in. All she wants to do
is get home. She's thirty-six. She's a thousand years old.
She thinks about grad school applications.
City of residency. Pretty cities of permanent residency
dance sleekly before her, as vacantly as dreams, as embers
going out in somebody's house, as the possibility
of becoming a medical doctor, or a virgin, or a Publisher's
Clearing House Winner, or somebody's mother, or somebody's
one true love, or a busty but slender clear-skinned
varsity cheerleader twenty years ago, with a frat boy's
ring going around and around her neck on a chain
that feels like warm fingers. She feels hollow,
feels like a sausage casing, a husk, a cortex
without the neo, a glue gun without the glue. She's empty,
she's Ginger Rogers spooling out on moth-eaten film
from Fred Astaire's velvet-suited make-believe arm. She wants
a puppy, wants to make jelly from scratch and put it
in jelly jars and put them in somebody's basement, wants to have
that dream again where Hannibal Lecter bites her toes
in the downstairs rec room of her childhood home,
while behind a tree in the backyard Danny Devito continues
to wait ardently, anxiously for only her, her suitor,
her one-and-only, short and lovely and warm as an old
old winter coat to be worn and taken off and hung
on some familiar hook that she knows, where she is
warm in a warm house in the city of her residency,
wants to wear that one city like it's true.

[handwritten margin notes: "Did this happen?", "section of the brain", "child like"]

More typical about stereotypes

HOW TO BE PERFECT (NOT YOU)

This is how to be perfect: to have picked a career (at least *one*
thing), your man, hatched two kids, have your own ingot silver metallic
   four-ton
Ford Fusion, your one glass of Domaine La Dame a day. The eggs in
   your basket.
This is what they do, the others (who aren't you) and you loathed it—

Not me, not, you said to people at bars, at reunions, you never were good
at math, or marriage, or a regular job, but you did serve beer and food
in places where you called men darlin', and went home with the last one,

and there were many days for short skirts, dollar bills, blender drinks,
the sloe gin fizzes too, the boys you passed through like they were
   minutes, who
you never missed (the men who never knew enough to know enough
   to think
to miss you), the panty hose, the décolletage, the broken-off high-heeled
   shoe,

the double shifts at bleary dead-end tables, but at day's end your own
place, the cheap shag, the tapered candles, the wallpaper's places peeled blue,
your grandaddy's pajamas, your mother's loaned sheets (and did she
   know how you

Complicated relationship w/ mother

turned from almost loving to always missing her, can she see you?)
   even though
you ran out the clock, the men, the minutes, the basketless eggs
   dropped down

the hatch, or in a blender, gone like the baby blocks that spelled out
   the future—
you as a woman, regular, a mother, your mother's daughter, a perfect
   picture—

not your life now, worn-in as the days, as flannel, as panty hose,
but lived-in and loved, as nothing you planned, but chose. *a ?*

think you will know of triumvirates
household gods, sometimes holy—
Jesus the Nazarene is a carpenter and my lover is a blind painter.
By day my painter paints brown verses
on woodstretched aching canvas.
By day he paints the things he would see from the eye of a storm or a needle
if he could see.
By day he paints the things faltering shutdown angels, the ones on heaven
probation, would say
if they could say.
By night his lips brush my brown cup on sheets whiter than Mary.
But the colors my blind painter paints do not matter. *(his work?)*
There is a woman always at the edge of his canvas
a silhouette with only the important things, *mother —*
breasts and a womb. She is the only important thing *Mary?*
but she is a shadow. She could be the mouth of a cave
or a scalloped shell or a seahorse. So
if I lie down with Jesus the Nazarene during the day
while he kneels by my butcher table grunting, grieving for me, giving up
blood and sperm, stretching me, if I lay my body down and splay my feet
and grasp a butter knife for want of his hand
and bleed, face staring into the red tiles of my kitchen
my church of the chablis glasses and paring knives and violent
red tomatoes, this carpenter, this shadow
when he leaves he will say, "Don't worry, I'll build you
another" — *Callous, like a man*
and if I lie down with my painter only at night
let him lay on me like he's smoothing a shorn piece of paper
we three will have made a beautiful wooden seahorse and painted it blue
    and white
the colors of Mary.

BONE

Eating chocolates last night in bed
I lost it. My own back tooth. Carefully
excavating it from a mound of sticky debris,
I studied the thing, the staccato, clean thrill
of pain arching through the new nook
of my gums, a thimble of blood pouring
in from the shift of this little failed bone
from me, and unexpectedly there was a thick loss
like childhood, like faith, like virginity
in the whole of my body that filled me up
like a potter's own faulty bowl, the sudden
less-ness of my whole, the unluckiness
of it, and the already distant missing bit.
Blood felt like a new and bastard christening, or
the tender violation of a soft imperfect hole.
I'd thought this, my own, my fossil,
would guide me always to vibratos of raptures
and rue, get me through the bitterest foods, accept
forever the wafers and the wine, and I grieved.
My own instantly frail teeth are skeleton keys
to a private doorway, *me*; the implacable boneyard
fenceboards gating in to flesh and out, again,
to ash; the gems on the chalice of tongue
and throat; faux diamonds that once
I thought promised *you will last, you will last.*
My own teeth were God's sacrament to me, His
white-hot cleaving to my flesh, and I clasped
them like the cross. Losing them is the folly
of rotting sacrament, giving his own body's
bread back, ungrateful, leavened and graceless.
I imagine at the end, or sooner, all these tiny
bones, the knotty little covenants I lacked
the care to keep, will fill up the cup of Christ
one by one, the brittle clink beckoning, calling
me, and I, a loosened sack, a slack unearthed
empty thing, will go back, limp as I came,
uncommunioned.

W E T

I want to leak all over the world,
the wet and tilted wheel, to squat on its axis
and spit my slippery fish, red and gasping
on the asphalt, under the streetlight. I want my life
streaked down my leg, to rain my seed on the ground
like a wine's sooty dregs. I want you to see that I am who
I say I am, an unsavory woman with her seasons undone. I want to lay
you, on a bed without a towel, without a curtain, without a good enough
reason. I want to wear a white dress stained with certain possibility,
    like an autograph,
like a river ripe with spawn, like a signpost, like a season,   / amp up the
like a dam come all undone.   / energy

← Female horse

AFTER THANKSGIVING

My mother asks me to rub her feet
and I sit on the couch
not rubbing her feet. She tried
to get an early ticket out of here;
they were all booked up. Paul,
pale in the cold kitchen,
is making strong coffee
with a Pyrex container and a red plastic filter
more durable than a heart is. She,
once a constellation of Ritz crackers and cotton balls,
brittles without her extra forks, her index cards
of Catholic-school-hand-written recipes,
her Band Aid expertise, her family of moons
gone away. I make a mess of loving her. Her face
turns to me
and is a bird fluttering
when I make a joke of the bronze lamé wallet
she just bought. She nests her sadnesses there
with its handy zippered pocket for prayers. On the table
sits a bowl of nonpareils I bought for her,
sprinkles holiday-themed. She goes outside
and smokes a Merit on the porch.
I can see each separate breath.

II.

TENDERLOIN RAINMAKERS

I'm drinking a warm Bud on the rim of this world
waiting for the hall phone to ring and watching
the old woman across the road in another residential hotel
wash her clothes in a cracked iron tub on the fire escape.

The dirty girl on the sill looks at me, sipping. I wring each sock
and each sock comes clean, makes a squall above the tub.
I hang them from the rail, tiny lightnings,
Christ's little soldiers. I don't judge sin but once I seen

Her old woman face is made of culverts, I bet one's from a husband,
one from a snakebite man that came later, one each from the gone-
away children.
The hurts hang from her like charms, the kind you find in the dollar bin
in the shapes of occasions that you hook round a chain.

she was wearing a shift with no arms that went just down to her hole.
I seen her ask a man do they want a date and I seen her arms
with their burnt-out circles. I am a watched secret too.
I want to put a cloth rinse around the hurt, Lord,

If the phone rang soon I'd be one round-the-world-grunt-and-wiggle—
   (God-why-won't-you-come-and-come-now)-now-pay-me-trip away
from the fix that means sitting on the curb smack outside
a hot-tub, free-ice johnny motel snaking the tube round my skin—

like that woman wrapped her hair all around You and got forgiven.
God why won't you come? Come now. I tip my water
into the street. A feral cat yowls its pain, wet tail
stuck right out like a baby's rattle or a baptized thing . . .

black lava blood bubbling out to make room for what that joy is, going in.

MICHELLE

Parked on the rock
of the kitchen floor that
the landlady put in herself, stone
by stone, uneven, smooth, buttery, I
talked—I guess loudly (it was a party, and
there was wine) with a woman the color of wheat,
even her eyelashes, and she was worried, she was
saying, about the execution coming that morning at
exactly 2:01. Her boyfriend is a prison guard at that place,
he is sensitive, speaks softly, collects prison poetry, and did I say
we spoke boldly? mainly because she was so bothered, not about the
   killing
exactly, but the 2:01 part, why 2:01 precisely? that extra minute of his
   waiting
past cure,
past expectation,
past a hope that goes
nowhere, spills straight
down your leg, that expectation
an extra minute you just can't hold it
in, the bladdery roaring in your head,
an implosion, sixty seconds too many,
a minute one more after the minute you're
held due, and I and the wheat-colored woman
sat and talked louder about it, and words grew out of us
and slipped, dropped like stones, like eight of them
exactly, one after another, each one landing with a smack
on a water from some great distance, like seconds, sixty
of them exactly, each one longer, louder, and then there was
the big baton voice of the prison guard, her boyfriend, or maybe
her fiancé, breaking the circle of two people talking wildly, steeling
themselves from the outside in: *Michelle, you are talking too loudly and
   annoying me.*
Things
stopped, maybe

it was a minute, maybe
he was just looking for something
to bind her there, to that brief
place, the way you wouldn't stop looking,
would you, would *he,* even a minute
after the minute you're held due, but
the wheat-colored woman wasn't surprised,
though I was, chastised, a wine-fuddled fool,
accountable, held due, on the rock in the kitchen
of my landlady, on that night where I spent words,
seconds you can't bring back, already fallen with
a terrible weight: Michael Ross killed eight women, well
two of them just girls, and so maybe he was already due, due
a long time ago, a stone falling into an endless well, maybe he
was due that extra minute of roaring, and maybe we all yell into the silence,
maybe we all do.

GANGES OPHELIA — Drowned herself

a woman with an empty bucket balanced like a hálá on her head
walks six miles to the river, away from the moon, skin dusky
as the copper she carries, noble as the barren promise
of drinking clean of a river, clasps hands to her head wrapped
with the tip of her sari sewn from rags which were once curtains
which were once colors, long ago bleached from suns streaming
through windows, now dusty from the miles. her hair is dusty,
her yoni, dusty. they are all thirsty. the wind presses her spine,
pushes her like a broom in the sand. she walks in the river.
her government has sold her river, like so many cases of cheap
coca-cola, has siphoned it off like gasoline from a brand-new
american car, has soiled it like an oily dishrag, covered in dirt,
in ash from floating cremains. she walks the river deeper, the water
rises, the bucket floats away like a tiny toy boat, a bulrush basket,
she closes and opens her eyes, sees the skin of her children,
pílá with poison, she clasps them to wet lids like colors
in an envelope, like precious stones or rags in a bundle. she walks
on, her eyes stream from the fumes of the river, she thinks
she sees the beautiful porous moon before her, a russet bindí,
drinking up the night, like a cup of black coffee.

You're a girl

alone, waiting at Fillmore and Geary to go to your Friday night
shift at the diner, but it takes two buses. The street is bare
except for the residue of castoff weekday skin. The dressed-up-go-out people
are already spandexed and preening with glamour to spare inside the bars.
You wait in your polyester pants, rubber waitress cleats,
logoed apron pressed and almost neat, shirt
soaped and rinsed in the rusty sink of the residential hotel.
A man with an open face like a blown-out paper bag
passes and asks you how much for a date. You sweat
inside your shirt which still wears the stains of last night
in the faint cursives of ketchup and coffee. The bus
won't come. You might be late. A phosphorescent tranny struts by,
says friendly, *Girl, you got any fruit? I would give my teeth*
for some fresh, fresh fruit. She laughs and wobbles past on three-inch heels.
Maybe you wish you'd gone with her to get some fruit.
Maybe you wish you'd gotten pounds of fruit with her and trussed up
your bare heads with apricots and peaches and pineapples and danced around
together like a couple of Carmen Mirandas and laughed so hard you forgot to stop.
Your shirt swells and falls, gives and takes like nuns
kneeling and getting up in their pews in a white church.
Some boys wearing windbreakers with the hoods skeined up tight
over their features walk by, looking for something to do. You look
down the street for the bus.

You're a girl

at the intersection of all-day Burger King senior citizen 90 cent coffee klatches,
and ten-to-five skin care places where they'll mix your shade to match;
at the crossways between desperation and those discos filled with manicured
    hopefuls
and Sour Apple Cosmos and couture clothes. You wrap your arms
against the wind against your coat. The boys stop to have some fun with you.

I don't know

if they hit you or what they said or even if it matters. I don't know if you got
    yourself
a left eye swollen like a rhubarb over a thumbprint smudge of earth,
or if the bus rolled by then, ready to stop, and the driver looked down

at you, backpack splayed out, contents roadkill, and sped up,
not wanting no problems on his last run in the Fillmore tonight.
Or maybe you just got on the bus, unharmed.
                              But you're a girl not there when later the people
who made themselves up in mirrors, glittered, hoped for something to
     happen that's new, spill out of last call, out of the doors of bars, empty cats
     stretching up and down,
licking empty grey streets, thirsty for the sidewalk and the violent white milk

*again, Finds
unexpected adjective
to resonate with
the entire scene*

JUST A SESTINA TO YOU, HONEY, LETTING YOU KNOW WHAT AN INTERESTING THING HAPPENED TO ME WHILE YOU WERE AT HOME RUBBING YOUR WIFE'S BACK

A martian fell out of the French windows into my bed last night,
he wasn't much different from you, honey, except the
hair in his nose was green not brown and
in his left hand he clutched a nine-inch satellite dish
(that's a little bigger, honey, than the one you clutch)—any
way he apologized for dropping in like that—I asked him to stay

you know, chat for a while—life, love, lipstick—so he did stay
actually he ended up spending the night
(in case you're wondering, honey, no, he didn't get any)
we just sat around thumb wrestling and well the
night was getting hot so I got us a dish
of butter pecan ice cream—he really lapped it up like a native, honey, and

then as we played a rousing game of Twister on my deck, he looked up and
noticed that the Christmas lights were still up, in March. They stay
up (I said) because I've got a married lover (that's you, my little dish)
so every day is Christmas, hooray! (honey I didn't say how every night
is Easter how you've crucified me baby) I could see he liked me, the
dish he held, he clutched a little harder and asked if there were any

chance for his little old martian self to experience any
earthly love. I have some single friends (I replied) and
they're pretty desperate (not like me honey) the
chances are good they wouldn't kick you out of bed—stay
with one of them and pretty soon one night
you'll get to try out that nine-inch satellite dish

in a way you haven't thought of; not many women get nine inches of dish
(I told him), matter of fact some women don't get any.
(that's where I'm lucky, right honey?) The hot night
grew cold, so we stopped hanging by our ankles from the deck and

came in and then I saw his suitcases (there, by the bed) You can't stay
(I said) My married lover could be by to see me any month now and the

place has to be empty. I might not even be here (I said) but the
(I was JUST KIDDING, honey) martian got huffy, packed up his dish,
asked politely to use my phone to call a cab, said he wouldn't dream of stay
ing and messing up my affairs. I asked the martian if there were any
thing else he wanted to know. Yes he said, How is life here on lovely
    earth and
I said Wake up—it sucks! Take me away, into the night

    (I said) but by then it was morning the sun was mooning us so any
    way he left (alone)
(taking his nine-inch dish) and I sat in my kitchen and poached some
eggs. Why didn't I go with him, why do I stay (but honey here I am,
    dishless and cold, waiting for you
to come any day any night)

A WATER SONNET

Jimmy, a plumber in the rough part of the Vineyard, will tell
of his love, his lust of water—letting it fly, streak clear
up and sheer and nude, like a light, like the flight before the fall—
bent from a downwards sky, it makes him hold wetness dear,
nectar in callused palms, its clean, diamond weight a fat tear
that brings him (a little way) to something sacred, there in humble
places, backyards, basements, and he'll drink down some beer
while he's telling you, blushing (even as he'll try not to tell), fumble
at the jukebox of the townie bar, but he will tell, he will, mumble
out the scenes, cool cement cellars and bathrooms made of granite
from Mexico and dug-down sinks of marble—nearer, more faithful temples
than any stained-glass church, and he'll whisper to you now, of the infinite
    tumble of water, heavy (heavier still, the knowing it will not stay)
    in his cupped hand, of this having God before him, before He
    slips away

INSIDE AND OUTSIDE

> Inside and outside her head, a billion, trillion stars swirled, circled and ex-
>   ploded. 9 million frogs croaked.
> trees fell in forests echoing down valleys. children were born and cried. the
>   flux of everything
> throbbed on and on. songs were heard in spheres within spheres, electric,
>   crackled sharp.
> She heard nothing. How could she when not once had she heard her own
>   heart beating.
>
> —*Duane Michals, words and portrait, "Inside and Outside"*

She's a woman. Alone, she's unpacked her one bag,
tucking sensible panties, one hardy white brassiere
with its three metal tongues and clasps in the back
into the plywood dresser flimsy as her pulse
beats the butterfly way it beats. The why of her being here
might be in her or might be out there. It's the kind of hotel
where you can pay by the hour if you wish, where men explode
like gunshots the way a woman feels it happen in her and falls.
But she's here by herself for the night, waiting a spell.
Inside and outside her head. 9 million frogs croaked. Trees fell.

She's a woman alone, which is something different
than a woman. The man who takes her picture
yes he is there but this makes her just more so. He's
a hunter, he needs only the capture, he sees a creature
in his crosshairs, he sites her in him, he wants
the lines of her, her skin pressed into a glossy paper thing
processed and delivered unto the fumes of darkroom
developer later, when he is alone, which is allowed
for him. But first he'll shoot, not caring: the flash, the sting. *sexual*
Children were born and cried. The flux of everything

makes a woman alone flinch who surely was not alone
when children were born and she soothed them

with blankets and soft breaths and shhhhs and baths
and her breasts, and men she loved and laid bare and laid under
and against, all still there tucked under what he sees, the cotton dress
whose wrinkles are hieroglyphs of where she's been
and who made her love like that and hurt like the hole
a gun makes through you and what it takes away
but the warrior wants only her flattened out, believes then
she heard nothing. How could she when

she's just a woman alone here in this no-tell place
and she's just a story, a form he wants to mold, to mount
on the wall, an opaque skin to add to his collection
of skins, to pose with her bouffant hair, her rheumy eyes,
and her silent face so blank that he can make a canvas
of her life as she sits there on the burst-out bedsprings
and doesn't know the why of all these things in her bursting too,
but as he packs up his camera she's only a matter
of what he can make of the thing, he can't hear her, he's thinking:
not once had she heard her own heart beating.

Harsh, watching

ON RECEIVING AN INVITATION TO DENBIGH HIGH SCHOOL'S TWENTIETH REUNION

I thought I was still on the wet earth
where you three, pockmarked and eager to live,
left me. Where you lay me after the pills
and the grass-green Mickey's Big Mouths, the ones
you whistled across to make the only man-made sound
and put me face down and made me the monster
with a mouth full of green grass, now
gorging on creatures close to the earth,
easy pickings with my one eye exposed.
That night you did it from above and behind.
Now I snatch shiny-eyed groundlings for breakfast.
I even ate a chick, veiny from the egg;
my mouth is a cave, a caul, my lure.   *— A monster*

I thought I stayed there, thin as a wood thrush call
and then thick with the undigested bodies,
but now I slice open the fat invitation to the Comfort Inn Suites
in Hampton, Virginia, and confetti rains loud on my lap.
In twenty years all but one hole has healed. If I went,
name tag glued to my husk, would you remember,
pure boys who turned my skin to slime,
the earth wet, and red, and the bottles' emerald stone,
and the doggie-style christening, and the crickets scream
over your hisses and the chiggers' bites
under your bodies writhing over me,
and milky cream luminous on the blades,
would you even remember me, the freckled serpent
who let you live, would you feel, even welcome,
the snap if it came, the cure?   *— The consequence*

odd metaphor?
Her cure?
Their cure?

32

SHOE, WORN

Look, there was this old woman—not old, really,
maybe forty and some spare change, but she'd lived hard
and had some shit luck all her life from graveyard jobs
and guys who left or wouldn't leave, and a tendency
to enjoy her schnapps after shift and then sometimes
get to dancing in bars, slow and sweet while the men's eyes
followed her over their well scotches, and so her face showed all that
though she wasn't all that old but you know how life can get.
And sometimes she didn't have a place to stay, until
the time she took up residence in a men's Timberland — *creative*
Fleecelined Nubuck Boot, Color: Wet Sand, that she plucked
off the stiff foot of a giant and dead crack addict
lying at the bus stop on the corner of O'Farrell and Jones
in the Tenderloin in San Francisco where the plumper
hookers have their stroll (while the trannies strut up on Larkin
where they sometimes do their laundry at the all-night place
or stop in for a drink at the Mother Lode when it's slow or cold,
and the skinny bitches who get all the prime trade work all the way
up on Sutter or Post). Anyway, these O'Farrells had already
set about emptying the man's pockets—they were very, very efficient,
and where he up and gone he won't need it—but also very squeamish,
which is why they chose not to untie the big shoe lest they touch
the cold foot and stain their fingers with what it feels like
to be gone. But this woman, who already knew that kind of cold,
took the shoe and went all the way to Golden Gate Park,
where the cops are pretty lenient about the people who squat there.
And the woman—damned if she didn't, finally, feel like she had a place.
She loved that shoe. It was warm, it was waterproof,
and after a generous application of Dr. Scholl's powder,
almost like new, like no foot had ever been lost in there.
She felt found, and that helped the sadness
she'd had ever since she lost her children to social services,
because everybody makes mistakes, but she came home
from work to the shoe after every shift almost, and she had a cat
and that cat, yellow ears cocked, would listen with her

to Billie Holiday on a sidewalksale LP record player, and wait
for milk, which she gave him always, and the milk in the dish
of the cat looked like the morning's going-away moon that shone
on the shoe where they lived, and she wore her life that way.

means this is a
fairy tale

THE RUSTY NAIL

I half-loved her the summer we worked the bar, her face
laced with those lines, the finger strokes of work,
of winey evenings, of half-bad luck, of the cool hustle of loving
too much and not getting that back exactly the way she served it
up. That made her great at pouring, the non-expectations
well-met, the mother-love, the box of aspirin behind the tap,
the smoothness of serving weary men, their bikes lined up and locked
at the stand in the front of the lot, stacked, a sheaf of good intentions
stapled to criminal records. Good men gone and done some shit—Hell,
she fished a Saint Christopher's medal out of the toilet for some old fool
who'd managed it, let him kiss her soft lips cause that's what he needed
to do. I half-loved her for her hand down the john, her magdalenic peace,
her giving, come from knowing all about good intentions gone bad,
which she told me one of these nights after work, over flat beers
and counting whiskied dollar bills, said, half-defiantly, *Never*
convicted, said, *you can't put all that love in one place and not have it*
come out, come up, come back to you different from when you gave it.
She leaned into me, cotton pilling v-top revealing cleavage a ravine
mossed in shadows, in secrets (in sorrows, in some things lost), her breath
rushing over me with its eddying layers of liquor, of cigarettes, of deep
blood like rain, whispered, *they never did find*
them bullets, sang, *the name of the game is you take it*
like that, and she tucked that wad of bills
in her Jordache pocket, and I wanted to bury
myself in there, in her, my separate secrets dark
alongside that wrinkled fold of ones.

another woman

FOR JILL, WHO'S BLUE ON ACCOUNT OF SHE JUST BROKE UP WITH HER LOVER, AN ASSHOLE DOCTOR FROM ACROSS THE WATER

You keep a stash of hardware magazines handy on the kitchen table.
You rub an index finger over each page of tools like they're porn.
You own a nailgun in the cellar that spits out the souls of old boy-
   friends.
You fish with nothing but a pole, your bikini, and live men as bait.
When the Shop-Vac breaks,
     and the boys fall away,
        the last bass is caught,
           the tools flaked with age—
there'll still be you, Jill, hair grey with sand,
you, chugging jug wine and bald guys and
   pitchers and pitchers of souls of men
         and all the sea's jismic spray,
you, who seduce the thin horizon in the flimsiest array,
   who weep the aubade,
     flirt hard with the stars,
         slingshot the sun until it sinks into the bay,
you, who strip off your thong and fuck the sky,
   rip off your top and shimmy around
     each power-sawed edge of the day.

FIREFLIES

October 29, 1982, a girl in too-tight jeans is walking the curb
of a darkening road in Newport News, Virginia. She is holding
a paper bag stuffed with things: a pack of Ho-Hos,
a Christopher Newport Community College sweatshirt,
eight-track tapes of Steely Dan and the Electric Light Orchestra.
These are meant to hide the bottles she stole, now nestled
at the bottom of the bag. She feels them in the crook of her arms
just like the buggy eyes of an upside-down baby. The road
is darker still, except for the winking of fireflies.
Any other night she would fear and hate them.
Their glamour and pizzazz. Any other night she would
hold their lights out to be sarcastic, a judgement. Any other
night she would want to stuff them in a jam jar
just to show them who's the boss of who, jabbing pen holes
in the aluminum lid for the terrible mercy of air. Tonight,
though, she is a curb walker, a spandex tightrope girl.
She is lit up inside just like the fireflies, just like a spangly harem
dancer or a string of Christmas lights, on the 29th day
of October, 1982. She has plans of making love tonight
with the boy who has sun-colored hair, who has no problem
with her big bones, who has a basement room where the light
is very dim. She wonders if he will lick her breasts
before he puts it in, and if so, should she moan. She wants
to go ahead and become a magical sex creature, wise
in men and weight control and eyeliner and what is happening
and what will happen. The Great Pumpkin, the orange
family Volkswagen, slows to a stop just behind her. Its brights
are on. I'm riding the curb, she sings to herself. I'm a straight
stepper. I'm a sharpshooter. You can't chase me, you can't
catch.   Decades later it's the funny story she tells around tables
full of after-dinner flotsam and crimson glasses of wine,
adding quirky details like whiskers on a long-forgotten cat.
I mean, I was wearing a *beret*, she adds, to shouts of laughter,
shaking her head in wonder at the story of the Night of Definitely
Not Getting Laid for the First Time. Who did she think she was,

[handwritten margin notes: "harsh / Frightening reference" and "girl-like"]

she says. She is careful always to put air quotes around Making Love.
They all laugh knowingly at Daddy shaking her like an upside-
down baby, so that the bottles from the bag were smashed on the curb.
She says, ruefully, *Literally* busted. Then someone tells another
family story, and she presses the pads of her thumbs in her eyes,
sees the flicker of spots, the thrown lights. She can see the red tiles
of the kitchen on the 29th night of October, 1982; she can see the carton
of milk on its side, spreading out like a caul. The contents of an aspirin
    bottle
settling in her tummy, a nest of white doves. She can see the man
in the bright white of the upstairs bathroom, picking up her torn-off,
plus-sized, stretched-out red panties, putting his nose in them, inhaling
its folds, a burning and beautiful bloom. She can see fireflies.

DORIS

for Memory and Oxford

"Apart from her roles as wife and mother, Doris did not play a large part in
the stories of Greek mythology."
     —*anonymous online source*

She was a type, all right, an Okie from her daddy's side,
when she met Nereus, maybe even a little flashy looking,
the bright penny kind that goes away with the wear
of that kind of particular female currency.
But she was a work-nymph for her husband,
bearing him fifty to ninety-two Nereids, according to Wikipedia,
which cannot really be relied upon for reliability.
But the point, maybe, is: all girls, all the way from Agave,
a slow-witted thing who later ate her baby, to Halie,
who either had ox's eyes or eyes of onyx. See again,
Wiki. The final of the brood was Thoosa, wild, the life of the party,
being last from the womb, girlfriend of Poseidon, never married,
a looker, a little loose. You have to wonder if all these female parts,
hysterical seahorses in search of a mooring, was why Nereus
kept shooting his nebulous griefs Doris's way, in hopes
of just one boy and heir, even after she lost her pretty figure,
took to putting on the first orange-trimmed caftan
she could lay her hands on mornings, trapping her uncombed,
un-conditioned hair in a greasy scrunchie. He'd scooch up
in the marital bed, year after year, and assume the missionary.
He only pretended to care: he had a second home, and
you try comparing with your husband's mother
if your husband's mother is the Earth.
Doris cared for her girls, though—think of the cooking:
cast-iron pots of clams and spaghetti,
the ordered epic rows of tuna fish sandwiches on wheat.
The dishes. The ironing. The boxes and boxes
of Costco maxipads. But each girl came of age and each one came

of loyalty, that fierceness a girl feels, that lust for her daddy.
And, think of all that blood, the way the sea smells
with its smashed rocks and salt rills and creatured bodies,
and each year a daughter swam away from Doris.
If you had a falcon's view looking above the night Aegean
you might see the steely glow of all those undone clothes-hooks
    differently, shining all in the dark. Think of a love like hers
    naked that way, looking like just so many disordered stars.

Tragic

III.

PIED BEAUTY

Glory be to the guy who invented Missouri for money,
with its plateglass heat, its thick-tressed storms,
its power outages, its broken water mains;
glory be to these broken-up brick stoops full of women who sit
calicoed, bandannaed, laughing and fanning at their men
making finger v-signs with light and dark roughened hands
who pull in from the Shop 'n Save and haul out silver bags of ice
from their Ford F-lines and pass them around;
glory be to Cedric's Fish Fry for cooking up everything
over a lit trash can before it all goes bad, glory to the beer
to be drunk while it's still cool, glory be to the E felony
of freeing the over-full hydrant, feeling the loose damp shirt
on the body; glory be to wearing nothing much, dancing with strangers,
glory be to somebody's six-pack of D batteries, for the flashlights,
for the boom boxes blaring the bleats of poetry, a band called pain,
glory to the little girl with her doll tucked football-style under her arm,
its boy hair crisped sleek in the middle, two like waves meeting each to each,
glory to her mommy, whose feet hurt, who's home now   _sudvent
whose love for this girl in this place makes her skin feel raw and soft; 1 one ?
glory for half a moon that haloes everybody the same this night
for the nest of debris and leaves we rest on, and later, in the hot dark,
while I wave a lazy magazine, glory to the found matches you touch
to our Jesus and Mary industrial candles, lighting up
your sweat-dabbed glorious face;
para que no me atormenten de nuevo sino que seamos salvajes en la gloria del
    espiritu santo.
Praise this.

So they no longer torment
no unless we are
savages in the glory
of God

WET 2.0

I wanted to make this a wonderful class, I type to my kids,
but sadly, I have failed. I click Send. I should have learned long ago
never to write what is supposed to be an apology after two and a quarter
glasses of Vinho Verde—not to lovers or used-to-be's and especially not
to a class of hopeful baby poets who spend their quiet time hunched over
wafer-sized Sony laptops thinking of new ways to say pussy when
it's spring and they really should be out there getting their hands wet—
I should have said dirty.

> DIRTY! You write in the margins of my manuscript,
> all that piss and milk and menstrual fluid flooding the work. It
>   bores me,
> you write. Can't you think of a more delicate way to express your
>   femininity?

Sally forth and fuck each other, I want to say
to my roomful of students. Do it against a tree
with the new buds around, tiny as toes,
and the wet earth making room around your bodies,
but the professionality I have to put on along
with the uncomfortable pairs of panty hose
precludes me.

> To you, though, I just want to say,
> —again—cunt and titties and holes and woman.
> Yeah, you, squatting in the margins, preferring
> to talk of sacred amber and stone altar and Nijinsky,
> croaking like a disapproving Canadian frog
> with your cock and ball-point penmanship, I want to tell
> about things that happen when your mouth doesn't form
> the hole *No* on the rocks in Marin and then you spill out
> so much that you're wearing Depends for a week
> and when you touch, your finger comes up poison plumeria,
> wet bright milk from a cup. I want to talk about squamous cells
> and their link, they told me, to previous female sexual hyperactivity,

[handwritten margin notes: "Introduction / diction / old fashioned / awkward / instructor-ly" and "look" with arrow]

44

and hey, while I'm at it—
                    to you, too, over there,
wearing your height-enhancing Texas cowboy boots
and your is-it-big-enough neurosis like a grin—
I most emphatically do *not* want to say: Auntie Flo,
or paper-covered cervical examinations in sterile rooms,
or monthly visitors or weekly douches or mammary glands,
or smooth-shaven mons venuses on the half-shell, or
feminine protective sanitary napkins, not even if they have wings
built in the sides big enough to fly, not even goddamn then. Yesterday,
one of my baby poets was sick and he asked me to feel his forehead,
and I almost did it, I swear I almost did but I failed. Did I fail you?
Have I mentioned how another kid came to me crying, *he left me,*
he finally did, and she spent the night on my couch? When I woke,
thinking of nothing but coffee, I saw spots there and marks on the
    cushions
where, in her night, she was trying to scratch the way through, and
    standing there
in my flannels, eyes curdled from sleep, I saw that it was wet.
        And now you   (because what in this good and green earth
        have I to protect you from)   want to know why I'm made of wet?
            I'm made of mother, baby. Come on,
                let me show you
                    my beautiful filth.

45

Rhyme

600-LB MARLIN ELUDES

the boy on the boat, his lure and slick line,
and the beast, streaming blue, a wet palette
of blues, dancing the blues, refusing the bind,
centenary migrant, flouting men, bait, intent,
intransitive, needing no one, grows intense, full-blown,
now rises the firmament up through the green lamplit fissure
of home, rides the mezzanine of waves against sun, made stone
for a moment, brighter than forever, arcing teasingly sure
between God and what man is, a one-word sentence, a No
without an object, a
      Not yet, I am old, archaic, nomadic
an atheist of God, a warrior, bold, I who have lived below,
a hedonist, a horny fish, having eaten well and known ravishments
and the dailiness of blue, the aching lovely spawn, I will not anchor this
life yet. Boy, this is our curse-gift, a cracked-open door, a fissured palingenesis.

spiritual rebirth

PUB POEM

If I hold my breath for a million ebbing years, little oyster
waiting my tables, fighting the tide, swimming to hope
and still I can't open you up, love,
I'll marry the fat red tomato
I got from an infatuated farmer who waits pleasantly
with knife and fork to eat me.
I'll marry the warm brown York, where naked swimming
is like breathing, a priority, and only as dangerous
as the soft-shell crabs slipping away on the sandy floor of the river.
I'll marry my worn work shirt, stained with Corona and crab cake
and sweat and a little smear of cocktail sauce like a margin.
I'll marry each lonely marine I wait on,
he and I will picture a possible me, painting my toenails
bloodred in a trailer, waiting for him,
for the slippery click of the lock;
knowing it now, we look away.
I'll marry the teasing moon whose bright vowels dance on the water
like the Yorktown Slut, promising everything,
sighing, before she slips away
what if, what if.
I'll engage my boss on his boat in thoughts of bra straps
and panties and other wistful trappings,
which become, like breathing, a priority.
I'll marry each barnacle I scrub
bare, barely staying afloat,
while the bass slip away past the rockabye boat and the waves whisper
dive under, dive under, seduction is rare,
seduction is hope.
I'll marry the Pub, and slop ice-cold mugs of beer
onto men whose eyes seem to say that I, too, am replaceable.
My sneakered feet will slip, I'll wed the salted floor that way—
slide into the sun and marry the day.
I'll marry the bent mirror in the back
where I pin up my marmalade hair
and stare at lips as red as cocktail sauce

the round everpresent planet of mouth
and fragile freckled arms who miss the man who slipped away.
I'll marry my beautiful brown teacher whose letters,
which say angst is my downfall, I read on the sneak
on a Budweiser box amongst the dead clams and unconsummated
    lemons
in the back of the Pub; I'll marry my downfall.
And if I fall down a hole as big as the Chesapeake Bay, big as my whole
yummy heart, today's Special of the Day,
I'll marry it.

FIRST COMMUNION

Mother when I was so small I was still
you (only with big eyes)
you brought your fragile claws down
over the dinner wine
over the pastel ladies home journal tablecloth
over your husband's disciplinary roar
onto the sullen crystal dish.

Burgundy ran sideways
down through the curtains down through the floor
and over us the gentle Lenten palm leaves rocked
green above the door. Daddy drove.
The emergency room door looked tiny from the parking lot.
I would never fit into it and I didn't. I stayed where I was
the way little girls do, behind the crystal windowpane
of the station wagon waiting and tracing my name in the dew.
When you came out, all cotton fragile corners and dark smudges,
you had four wire ribbons
in your wrist, one for each year I was born.
I wanted to climb back into you.

Later you lay in another room
with the door open, flooded, silent
under daddy's big legs,
and I crawled myself
under the green fronds
into the kitchen's glassy secret mess
into high sweet sacrament that stank of blood and wine
and I cut myself on a piece of your shining eye.

49

HOLDING

I have waited so long for you. When I was three I tried to get to you,
cunningly, two Dixie cups attached at the bottoms to a cord unstuck
from my father's office phone, me in a blue polka-dot swimsuit, two
piece, stomach puffed out like a fat white cumulous balloon. My luck

didn't hold. I kited the cup up to you hard as I could from the long shore
at Hog Island beach, but I threw like a girl, and you couldn't reach.
It floated back like a waxen Moses basket. At ten I tried again, laid on
    the floor
like nuns in movies. The linoleum smelled of dogs, fried things, and
    bleach.

In my twenties, frankly, I looked for you in some down and dirty places:
in fraternity rooms, in the bottoms of bottles, in diners slinging plates
    of spaghetti,
in the plastic backseats of Toyotas with boys whose sweaty and
    desperate faces
I searched for the stain of stigmata, or something unworldly, or any
    kind of holy.

I've been on hold so long, longing, so, if you get this, please, *please* let
    me know,
because I need you and I'm gonna let go, and if you're coming for me,
                                    you're coming too slow.

THE SHAPE OF HER

She's tired, unsteady at the end of a beery night, still standing though,
still wary, haunches still ready, she's ready, she's a deer. Not really.
She's a woman still wearing her little cotton three-days-straight black dress
revealing the shape of things; she's wearing *howdiditgettothis* like a corsage,
some mute flower hanging limp, some numb feeling. But when she says
    something
she means it and this is the shape of her that makes her afraid.
She leans against the windowsill, feels its outside breath seep
under her nails. She feels like she's been standing like that for days
like a child waiting for a shot, like a stranded motorist, like the blindfold
feels when it's wearing the poor bastard in the courtyard, like a pounded nail
in a fellow on a cross. She feels like she can't stand it. Sometimes
she makes the midnight phonecalls to that man who fucked up her life
that time—he's very old now. She says, *Remember when you said*
your payback for killing me was gonna be prostate cancer? She says,
Got it yet? the hiss of years between them, the toenailed stretchmarked
    phonecord
pluming up like smoke. Soft click. She heard he changed his number, or
    rather,
the operator told her, *Unlisted,* even when she says she's his sister in Wis-
    consin,
their mother has had a bad stroke. She hears the doubt emanating
from the operator who must field these graveyard-shift pleas
all the goddamned hands-free headset days of her life—a priest, a confessional,
a receptacle—how do they even stand it? And anyway, she fucked up
with that story, 'cause the man is very old, he wouldn't have a mother
who'd have a stroke of anything, not that the operator would know.
She sighs. Soft click. She can't believe she doesn't get to call the man
who royally fucked up her life. She says *Christ.* Then she doesn't say
thank you, but she really really means it. — Not sure

51

BAKE

You bake like you like to live, imperishably, even in this 100-degree heat,
with gusto, your giant's fingers churning into impossibly moist yeast
    and wheat,
unceasing in the florid red backroom of an impudent French bistro,
    your hands
running the dough over and over again, making it flow, roll, yield and
    go, dance,
ready to rise to the occasion, be consumed. You make things impend;
    you, sheathed
in kitchen-nicked skin, finish things off that way. You drink water,
    vivid with relief.

You bake like I want to live someday, the me who watches every minute
go by, impatiently, each a drab one-act play; me who imbeds a forever
    dent,
an ache in the drab olive couch; me, a slob, a loafabout, an impatient
    girl who
coils around the sheen of a cool drink, a lazy serpent at a shady,
tree; me, who sees the summer bleeding out watercolor, who reads her
    tea leaves
of sweat, me who waits for you, my impasto man, impassive, serene,
    vivid with relief.

TWENTY

At two a.m. twenty years ago he could tell me what she looked like
twenty years before, her dress the color of smashed mandarins
straight from Ly Nhan but still a delicacy to him. They drank in the GI bar
then went to her room, her mouth still wet, pursed like a wound.
She had skinny legs the color of soft earth and knees that clicked together
like poolhall balls, his boomboom broad. Love is a thing that spools away
easy as a coil of copper wire; afterward he lost his job back at New England
Telephone & Telegraph, halfway up a pole he couldn't stop sweating at the way
the great cables tattooed the sky. At two a.m. I learned the way the years roll
    back,
bandages from shirts, meals ready to eat, soaking rice husks cooling beer, an
    arm
picked out of a bush by a road, and back before that, ten years before that,
the sidewalk outside his walkup, a ducktail punk talking pussy and ass
with Mikey and Joe, to look up and see the soiled bedclothes his mother hung
like a flag from his room, the stain a burst sun and the whole thing fluttered
in the wind, there are wars. Dirty smoke at Loc Ninh, a long-ago cigarette
    burn
on a palm. (How big are your titties now, he asked me twenty years ago.)
Years: the bottles of Jack Daniels, the smooth bone dice in the hand, the child
whose key won't fit in the lock, six half-zipped Glad-bagged men in the back
    of a truck,
the fear when a breeze goes still. She was a real doll, my uncle said at two a.m.,
my juice girl, and I picture her peeling out of the orange dress in one motion
forty years ago, the way a nickel-bladed pocketknife pulls down the rind.

maybe

STONE

I am the domestic.
I am the dust and rock and plaster
that clings to your bare flesh
in this new apartment in summer, stubborn,
unrelenting, despite my hot water and Pine-Sol
and paper towels and hands and sooted knees.
I am the crusts of burnt-out bread when you lift up
the ten-year-old toaster, I am the fingerprints of bleach
on your famous black Calvin Klein shirts, clean going nowhere.
I am the spilled-out impure grit, and laundress of it.

I am the put-in-orderer.
I am the one that will smooth closed your books,
pluck your shorts from the floor, indecent, gaping,
tuck them in, make them well. I am the girl
who will want to lift you up, cuddle you,
swath you, drop you, wash you under the water,
run you over the border, take you somewhere
against your will you want to be with me,
deliver you anemonied from heat and grief and wear.
I am your hurt, I am your protector.

I am the small stone,
what you thought was a small stone,
that soon finds its home and nestles right into your foot—who
told you not to go barefoot on the edge of the Mississippi?—
that you learn to walk anew around. I am the one too
who will root you clean and bind you in bird's-egg white.
I am your ragged tooth, I am the mouth it lies in, the lovely shame.
I am the small bright flame that lights up the front yard grill.
I am the smoke that floats up from the yard,
dirty and fragrant, of ash and fish and cumin and tar
that makes the air here humid as a door. I am the want
that makes you get up and take it and you don't know why,
that makes you poor enough to forget about all that,

that makes that Schlafly beer, flat and smooth, funnel down your throat,
that makes you hate and love this place hard. I am the shapely
tornado that shears and the one small lawn chair it leaves,
when it leaves, awry,
the coal-eyed animal who burns in you,
your fast, your feast, your Missouri, your supply.

LOVE SONG: ANNIVERSARY

I keep wanting to break him. I'm crazy why
and I haven't felt this thin wild string twang
through throat and cunt and toes for thirty years
since I gave up Ken, molested, left him shorn of his
horsehaired well-coiffed emptied head, dumped
by the side of my Holly Hobbie sheets, torso
still intact, still anatomically effete, unable
to harm the girl but, fuck, unable to meet her needs.

I keep wanting to break him. I want to move him,
this man I bed so surely, this guy who lays me flat
with accuracy, anatomically 3-D, all there, heavy
scrotum, lean-to dick, matt of hair. I want
to grab him by the shaggy nap and yank him,
make him leave, make him careen away from me,
flee on flat real feet with bony surgical-case
(perfectly) arthritic knees from his erroneous
devotion: me, with my flappy old-woman
tits, broken cervix, wet selfish imperfect pussy.

I want to jiggle him till the peanuts improbably
fly, piñataed free from his wholly human head,
Styrofoam evidence of those awful (beautiful)
thoughts of me, the old wife, the stamped and decaded
life, the stained sheets, the slightly limping (lovely)
we. I keep wanting to shake him, wrestle his arms away,
break his steady stay, twine his hands that hold me still hold
me still.

EUCHARIST

they shall look on Him whom they have pierced
My father was a guarded man, wore wool pajamas
even in the summer and scratched at them like a sore.
I never saw a naked man until Jesus at the altar, on
the cross. I moved to Him up the aisle with fear, long
fasting, and longing, too,
take, eat, this is My Body
To taste the salt of His bread, His unleavened flesh
his head turned to one side in perpetual piety or shame
as if, in dying, He refused to meet the gazes of those
who would hail Him with stone, nail Him shut like a burning
flame in a sealed room of marble
drink of it all of you for this is My Blood which is poured
To suckle the Lord's son's lanced and open side of reddened
water, sip secret at his sacred hands and heels, the accidents
of blood and wine, like venom from a vein, like beautiful thunder,
like sin to balm, to press my lips to His vinegared lips, to make
my mouth the sacristy, opened wide to take the poison in me from
Him and so to heal His sores
Eli, Eli, la'ma sabach-tha'ni? — My God why have you Forsaken me?
why, why have you made me so love my Savior? I will want, I will
guard, I will wait like these sumptuous grieving Marys, until a time
I am cursed or carried up to You, to soar or be shut in, unconsummated,
like an insubstantial candle
in the rock — Not SWC

57

HYSTERIA

When my mother had her things took out
I beat up this fat girl at school and lost my virginity
all over the daisy coverlet in my room
and once more outside the house, by the spigot
—same yellow underwear, two different
boys—because most everything's got an expiration
date. I never visited the hospital where they took
those things out but when they let her home
I looked in at her bed while she was doing stuff
that made sounds in the bathroom
and I'd stare at the place where her head had been
on the pillow, bare as an egg cup,
and I'd smell the basket of bloody pads
and later her and Edna, those two
sat at the kitchen table, my mother
in some ratty shift and Edna who said,
with the tip of her cigarette burning
like the point of an exclamation: I don't know
but I wouldn't let them take nothing out of *me,*
and right about then the jelly jar of juice
broke all up in my hand:
it run red, like a river it run.

SPAIN

My lover and I, we're having red wine and pork tenderloins
with some people we really don't know at the kind of restaurant
named after a good Manhattan number. The woman beside me
touches my sleeve. Her husband left her with the baby three years ago,
or maybe it was ten. *It's hard for him,* she sighs, *he can't get to a phone
to call his daughter.* She leans into me. *He's in Spain.* My lover and I,
we don't have any.

I picture this man under a hot sun, in the siesta in summer, in a cabaña,
with some sweaty restorative Spanish drink in his hand, maybe a sangría,
or some days it's a frígola, with a pretty paper red and yellow umbrella,
recovering, dozing, past three o'clock, past three years, past forever,
disfigured from the closeness of hot baby breath and jars and jars of Gerbers'
laid out in the refrigerator with military preciseness, and vaporizers
and spit and piss and things that leak, things that leak all over the apartment
and too much into yourself, and poop, poop over everything, like
a brown paper bag over the sun, poop that never stops, like muddy
puddles from a three-day rain, like a factory job, like a fever, like he never
believed it could be.

Later, it's coffee, and I look at this woman next to me, and I picture this man
      as he
pictures asking for a phone but the phone it's so hot in Spain it would burn
his hand if he touched it, or maybe that hot baby breath would burn his face
if he felt it, electric shock across the wire, sounding a little older, a little more
desperate, lisping forever words in high frequency, words like *daddy,* and
      apple,
and *up,* and *more,* and *me.*   — a little heavy-handed

59

MEDUSA'S LOVE SONG

It used to be that I longed for my family.
Two half sisters so close they split an eye
and shared it like two halves of a jagged
crystal egg, but neither ever held it up
to glance at me. The townsfolk turned to
face the walls on hearing my heavy feet,
my hissing hair. Once, so desperate, so crazy, so
needing for someone to look at me, I grabbed
an old man's cheeks and stared. He
cracked in two like a marble baby.
Only in dreams did the people meet my gaze.
I began to sleep all day. In truth,
I was lonely. So grateful when he
finally came for me; when he sheared me
away from my shoulders like a prize, like
a dowry, and flew on feathered toes
with me. I felt, for once, treasured. And he,
so proud, placed me up front, right on his shield,
like a rocket's tip, like a locket, like a ruby, like
somebody's beautiful baby rocking fiercely
in the armor of his arms. Now I ride him
like a worn-in saddle, like a silver dolphin
diving face-first into a sea of clouds.
He wears me like a candy necklace, like a wreath
of lily, like the skin of *yes this is my true face,* and
the snakes stream like lovers furling behind me.
He sees through his shield; he sees through me.
I cry when he cuts his soles on the stars, and
his blood and my tears land and make small horses.

[handwritten annotations: "echo with her mom's cutting herself"; "her head?"; "Q:"; "often wild metaphors at a poem's end"]

60

SHELL

Since you been gone I like to ride my bike some nights
over to the Shell Station, the one on Brentwood
just a couple blocks from the Little Flower Church.
I like to move through the bright aisles just like
I'm anybody else who's got a right to be there.
They sell Trojans and Lifestyles and Pleasure Plus
lined up on a metal tree like birds in paradise.
There are rabbit-footed keychains that smell
of being next to the hot dog Ferris wheel, sure
to bring you luck. They got Sour Skittles,
Hostess Snoballs, long strings of Laffy Taffy,
Rainblo Pops in primary colors,
Jack Steak's Peppered Beef Flavored jerky.
They have laminated mass cards if you need to say sorry
to God, and dashboard Marys made of painted clay,
and candles of Spanish Jesús or African Jesus,
with some psalms wrote right on the backs in other languages.
One has a living heart stuck all over with nettles.
For a quarter I get me an atomic Fireball and suck on it then
drink an energy juice real fast so you feel like a rock star.
Not someone who's been left. Less than a buck you can buy
a 64-ounce soda cup and fill it up with Dr. Pepper
and it's so big you have to tip it up in both palms,
cradle it like a cold frosty Styrofoam baby.
I had my way, you'd be up there way above Deb at the counter
and I might say, Deb, slide me that man down here—
no that one, there, first from the back. Casual-wise,
I might add on a box of Kotex, some two-dollar scratchers,
a pack of Nutter Butters, all broken up the way they go.
I'd pay her in money made of sow's ears and conch shells
and all the suffering I been having lately. Give it all away.
Deb, she'd slide y'all in a plastic bag and I'd walk out
swinging that bag high as anything, a rocket on fire
or a jungle gym swingset or a hurt like a toothache that rolls you
all the way upside down the way they do.

At home I'd set you on the kitchen table,
unwrap you, unscrew you, drink and eat you
till there wasn't nothing left. You left and
I'm raining from the inside out all the time now
like the wax paper cups at the Shell you put your Slushee in
when it starts to sweat from the heat. My heart
is all wrapped up in the kind of weeds with flowers that sting.
And I'm broke like that candy heart necklace you brought me:
when I tried to put it on the string flew,
I figure it's like you when you ran away. Did you know—
Nutter Butters start out as all one cookie,
then they mostly smash them down there at the factory.

deceptive

A MARRIAGE POEM

to her who read me that

My mother is somewhere in baggage claim at 11:08, lost maybe, uncol-
   lected,
having missed her first flight because she couldn't get off the on ramp,
and Paul is circling T.F. Green International Airport, which isn't large
unless you consider the state of Rhode Island. Inside everything is indeed
green, and suddenly, there she is. *I know who you are, said the baby bird.*
I see her in a sea of aquamarine waiting chairs, and I think
as she gets up, you are old and ill and you are not my mother.
I am getting married tomorrow and the chairs are stained and remind me
of a methadone clinic. I notice she is wearing a yellow velour tracksuit;
I get her bags which are circling their own drain and carry them out to
   the Nissan
now idling with what they call my fiancé at the wheel. It's her birthday
   today.
Here she is, I say to the man I want to marry, and she says to me,
You finally grew into the bags under your eyes and I smile and remember,
You are not a kitten, or a cow, or a big thing like a jumbo jet or a crane,
and I want to get her drunk. We drive to a bar and grill by the water
and she orders piña coladas. I'm drinking Bloody Marys that taste like
   metal
and are good with their violent celery spears and rage. She says
I miss your beautiful hair, and I pick up a fork and put the tines
in my mouth, then I put it down and walk over to the bar and order
another strong birthday piña colada and I hate her for she is weak.
The waitress walks over with the piña colada singing "Happy Birthday"
though it is now well past midnight and no longer, technically, true.
We all sing and my mother claps her hands together like a child.
Like a child, she claps and claps, and turns her head to me and says,
No one ever sung that to me before.
Heart, you are flung like a bird
whose own heart beats a thousand times a minute. I am a child. She
   smoothes

my wet hair back, kisses my forehead, tucks in the sheets below my
    feet
because I have been afraid of the Toe Monster for years, and she turns
    the page:
*There she is, said the baby bird, but the boat did not stop. The boat went
    on and on.*

B.A.R.T.

Ro got three hundred from a man who would take me for a drive along the big rocks past Marin. The shapes were like seals in the dark with the waves licking them all over to make shiny skin. We got out and sat on the red rock and the man poured me rum in a plastic cup with creases from use so when I drank I looked at its side and saw my face split white with a scar and the more he poured, the more I laughed to see the face turn into an old woman, and he put his arm around me and I saw behind him the moon tuck tail and scram when he pushed me hard and later when I woke and picked my way along the rock and down the road a cabdriver just off shift stopped and picked me up and in his drop-down passenger mirror I saw Mars in me full of puckered pools and he took *blood?* me to his studio and I showered while the sea eddied red around my toes, and stayed for three weeks in his apartment and all he asked for was company and a little sex, then I rode the subway through the water after I robbed him blind. I do not die.

SMALL YAHWEH

The larkspur grow bold outside the coffee shop on Delmar,
loud and seeking something from out each burst-forth root.
If I were a priestess, or some minor goddess, not Beatrice,
not Laura (*l'aura, l'aura, whisper the monks in their gathering
breaths*) I would own divinity of these small diminutives, delphinia
tendrilling to reach me, and, too, the plums from their mothering
trees would fall to me, the hem of my robe eventually
flowering grape, grown heavy and satiate with purple prose.
I would grow soaked drunk and pregnant with love,
and I would not ask to love more, except half a hundred impertinent
oranges, burnt bergamot with the ache for faith, and then there
is the dew, whom I would let marvel up my thighs, denude
the orchards, and the wet would jewel me and plummet through me
glinting, gunshot through my sponged and pulpy heart,
and these votaries would trumpet me, carry me up, lay me
gently down, and when I and the larkspur and the fruited animals die,
others spring up and beatify the air from their pedicel lamps,
sing your sacred name.

WHORE

The first thing I did when I moved to Charlottesville
was flip through the phone book for whores. In this town, it seems,
there are no whores, not in the yellow pages or the white.
Usually you find them listed, alluringly, under *Outcall,*
or *Escorts,* or one time, in Philly, *Massage: West Pamela,*
The Girl Who's a Place.

At Silk and White Lace in San Francisco, if you gave the driver
a blow you only had to pay him half. Long time ago.
Now, every town I'm in I get in the old way of looking up
the working girls. Boy-girls, pretzels, all around the world—twice-
    girls. At Silk and White Lace in San Francisco, Carolyn,
the madam—same name, that's why the johns called me Cinnamon,
that and because of my freckles I guess—this Carolyn made me wear
pleated skirts and plaid socks and shiny mary janes and say
It's My Very First Time.
I'm not in that trade anymore,
which is fine, now that I currently reside in Charlottesville,
since apparently here there's no free exchange of goods for valuables,
but I've got to wonder about all those men taking that long car ride
over to Richmond, or even just going home, hanging up their coats,
sitting in front of the TV with a beer while the wife
waits like a wraith, or fires plates in missile formation at the floor.
I wonder too what all the whores do without their johns
in Charlottesville. Because some people, we have just the one gift,
you know? I have a daughter somewhere that I lost.

At Silk and White Lace in San Francisco, me and the girls would knock
a few back at the Royal Oak on Vallejo with its wide leather couches
and a fireplace and real live red-eyed-olive drinks.
I used to think this must be like what being in Greece would be.
It's funny the things you remember. Like the guy just come back
from Desert Storm that couldn't do anything. I just took
my slip off and turned round for him with my socks still
on, around and around, like a top.

PRAYER

At the Green Street Café it's too warm.
I'm having white wine and recovering
from an eye infection, watching
the red kettle that whispers wet breath,
its sides white with remembering
old water. The drops the doctor gave me
have coated what I see with a layer
of Vaseline. The people are made of gauze.
I'll stumble home and plait my soaking hair.
Water, watch me. Make a bet I'll live from this.

Read Arielle's article

ACKNOWLEDGMENTS

I would like to acknowledge and thank the following publications in which some of these poems first appeared: *The American Poetry Review, The Yale Review, Ploughshares, The Massachusetts Review, Georgetown Review, Mudfish, The Cortland Review, Cutthroat, Margie, Rattle,* and *Alehouse.*

"Pub Poem" was originally printed in *Kiss Off: Poems to Set You Free,* edited by Mary D. Esselman and Elizabeth Ash Vélez (Grand Central Publishing, 2003).

"Just a Sestina to You, Honey, Letting You Know What an Interesting Thing Happened to Me While You Were at Home Rubbing Your Wife's Back" was originally printed in *You Drive Me Crazy: Love Poems for Real Life,* edited by Esselman and Vélez (Grand Central Publishing, 2005).

"litany" was reprinted in *The Best American Poetry 1993,* edited by Louis Glück (Scribner); *The Best of the Best American Poetry 1988–1997,* edited by Harold Bloom (Scribner, 1998); *The Body Electric: America's Best Poetry from The American Poetry Review,* edited by Stephen Berg, David Bonanno, and Arthur Vogelsang (Norton, 2001); *The Hell with Love: Poems to Set You Free,* edited by Esselman and Vélez (Warner, 2002); and *Alta traição,* edited by Carlos Felipe Moisés (Unimarco, Brazil, 2005).

I would like to acknowledge the book *Are You My Mother,* by P.D. Eastman (Random House, 1960), from which I am grateful to borrow lines for "A Marriage Poem."

Much gratitude goes to the Smith College Poetry Center, my fellow Smith Ada Comstocks, and the Barbara Deming Memorial Fund.

My love and thanks to Roberta Rosenberg, Jay Paul, Mary Esselman and Elizabeth Ash Vélez, Ellen Doré Watson, Annie Boutelle, Dasiy Fried, Ernie Alleva and Lisa Leizman, Christa Romanosky, Mark Parlette, Charles Wright, Bill Oram, Michael Gorra, Carol Christ, Alfonso Procaccini, Elizabeth Harries, Barbara Kozash, Joe Danc, Gregory Orr, Rita Dove, Jeb Livingood, Adela Feran and Matt Wallace, Barbara Moriarty and her beloved Joe, Jim Dozmati and John Sielski, and my family: Bob Weinberg and Eleanor Wilner, Julia Williams, Medusa who saved me, and Paul Andrews, who saves me every day.